# LOVING LIFE

## POEMS OF LIFE

## LYNN BERCOT

LOVING

Do you know that I love you?
Do you care that I care?
Do you know all the things that I want to share?

Will you leave me tomorrow?
Will you go without trace?
Will I never again see your dear loving face?

Will it be raining in my heart
Till the memories fade away?
Or will a peace come to my soul on some far distant
day?

Is it raining in heaven?
Is its sky a darkening blue?
Are those stars a blazing trail leading me to you?

# THE ARTISTS

The writer's pen drops ink
Across the page I think
Like fleas and ants
In a free twisting dance
Shaping letters, words, stories
To free us from our worries.

The painter's brush enthralls.
On paper, canvas, walls
The colors dark and bright
Depicting all in sight
Or from this artist's mind
What essence he may find.

An artist who works in clays
Forms items to fill our days
With a tangible shape and feel
Full of memories special and real
That comfort your insides
Where the magic in you hides.

The chef provides at the very least
The most marvelous and beautifully special feast.
Concocted of fabulous flavors all blended
And with a lovingly creative touch tended.
The recipes based on remembered pastry,
Vegetables, meats and sauces so tasty.

The composer hears an inner song
Of note after note short and long.
High after low.  Low after high.
Reaching inside the heart to try
To bring out the melody made by tears
From all the challenges faced through the years.

The actor brings someone within to birth
A person to bring pleasure, pain, sorrow, mirth.
A new voice none ever quite the same
A rare child born of all who came
To help to make this special creature
From sigh to walk each unique feature.

# HEALING NIGHT


In the night there is a peace
A moment dark and still
A time of quiet thoughtfulness
That helps to restore our will.

# GRIEF IS A TIGER

Today's grief is a tiger stalking me.
Its eyes are bright with a greedy light.
Its raging hunger walking free.

I can feel its steps so very near.
Its fury moving where we passed.
Its growing strength producing fear.

This terror of the lonely night
Hides in the deep, dark, fevered mind
Brought out when I'm weakened by my fight.

But I'm rescued then by our sweet love
Still strong and residing within my soul
Like an angel guardian from above.

# GONE

Weeping, weeping deep inside
Longing for the past
Seeing scenes from yesterdays
When my fate was cast.

Listening, listening for his voice
Lingering on my name
Telling secrets shared by us
In our teasing game.

Waiting, waiting no sound comes
In those tones I know
He's not here to say the words
And I miss him so.

SEASONS

The dry, crisp winter has left the land
Life's no longer grey
Spring has come with the golden dawn
Of a green and glistening day.

When spring is gone and summer's here
The heat lies on the ground
Like a blanket on a soft, warm bed
Where peaceful rest is found.

Magic comes with the autumn cool
Green turns yellow, red and brown
Leaves blow and flutter, quake and fall,
Tremble and spiral down.

Winter comes cold and quiet again
With snow swirling in for a stay
The glittering, frosty stars shine above
As the trees seem to shiver and sway.

# TRACE

As I wonder through our place
I hear your voice.  I see your face.
A gentle touch upon my cheek
The tender moments that I seek.

But truly you're not there to see
Not the way you used to be
But sometimes just beyond my view
I swear I see a trace of you.

# SILENCE

We had that talk some days ago.
It was not over when we parted.
We walked away and lived our day.
We can't now finish what was started.

There were those plans to take that trip
Together when we could make it there.
But now that date will never come
And that's a place we'll never share.

There was a promise that was given
As our heated talk was ending
To fix that problem that was hurting
And bring about a needed mending.

So many things are left unfinished
Over now, without a choice
All these things stopped waiting for us
And ended with your silenced voice.

# ALL MY LOVING FRIENDS

Love is the simple magic of the soul.
Love is a music within that makes us whole.
Love is a pair with a matching, pulsing beat
That can become something special when two people
meet.

Laughter is a song of tinkling, trilling joy.
Laughter comes with discovering a new, exciting toy.
Laughter shared is wondrous for everyone it lifts -
And when it comes, treasure it as one of life's great
gifts.

Tears can be signs of joy springing from our eyes.
Tears can be the outward mark of deep and painful
cries.
Tears that band two people can help them
understand
The many ways that life is like an earthquake in the
sand.

And so we find we share so much while we are on
this earth.
It isn't hard for us to see how much a friend is worth.
They are a part of our love, our laughter and our
tears
And will share our beautiful memories all
throughout the years.

## SHADOW

Sometimes I feel your gentle touch
Or glimpse your smile I miss so much.
Or in the darkening night you might be
That shadow that's in front of me.

Look at my hand.  I know it's shaking.
It lies there waiting, freezing, aching.
You are not here to hold it tight,
To kiss my lips and say good night.

You cannot be here next to me
In the way you used to be.
Yet, you are not so hard to find.
You are always in my mind.

# MY HUSBAND'S DIAGNOSIS

Those days were like a waking dream
When time sped up then seemed to slow.
Those moments not a steady stream
But seemed to stop and stall and go.

I struggled through my thoughts awhirl
Like ribbons twisting, tangling, turning.
Fighting through the confused swirl
Of my emotion's painful burning.

My mind was screaming at the word
That gave no hope for future years.
The verdict was a sharpened sword
That tore my soul and loosed my tears.

## LOVE'S PATH

I remember in my teens
The singing, laughing of my youth.
Dancing around in tattered jeans.
Looking for clues to life's great truth.

My first young love was oh so sweet
And like a girlish dream.
It began amid the summer heat
With picnics and ice cream.

But summer turned to autumn cool
And I grew up that year.
By winter I felt such a fool
And the cost to me was dear.

I was angry, broken, hurt.
Hoping to find some healing.
I learned to laugh, sigh, and flirt.
Trying to protect from feeling.

But in crept a lasting, gentle love
With all its tender pain
Sent with blessings from above
Like a warm and cleansing rain.

And that's the love that lasted years
Through all our battles shared
Through all the memories, joys and tears
Because we have always cared.

## MY DOUBT

Word after word pounding in my ears
They echo within me bringing me to tears.
Pain after pain searing through my soul
Tearing at my insides taking such a toll.
Thought after thought flitting around my brain
Phantoms and demons - am I now insane.

# TEARS, MEMORIES AND SHADOWS

Tears like tiny droplets of pelting, pouring rain,
Falling - a symbol of my overwhelming pain
Sparkling like splintering pieces of glass
Like memories of moments I cannot let pass
Shadows like moths moving in the cooling night
Swirling, spinning, diving in the flickering light.

# DREAM WORLD

When I awake from a dreaming sleep
Where my love will always abide
I snuggle down in the bed so deep
With the feeling of you at my side.

And I hug your love so tight to me
Like a secret in the night
And think of things as they could be
In a world where all was right.

But I am not alone I know
As you lull me with your smile
We have that place where we can go
In a dream world for a while.

## SOME GOOD

I hear those words that people say
"Tomorrow is another day."
I know that every word is true,
But it's so much harder without you.

The days can fly by oh so quick
Or slowly moving tick, tick, tick
But as a traveler through the days
I make a difference many ways.

I can find a smile to share
And try to show how much I care
By looking for some good to do.
For all who are so lonely, too.

# A RAINBOW

There are no flowers without rain
No life without its share of pain
Sun and wind gives plants a chance
To cover the earth in a beautiful dance.

And I am like those delicate things
That water and light to this world brings.
And so, when life mixed joy, pain and fears,
God gave me a rainbow through my tears.

# YOUR SHADOW

Your shadow walks beside me
And tells me you are near.
It holds my hand and guides me
And takes away my fear.

Your shadow always guards me
And makes me feel your care.
I feel your love towards me
When they tell me no one's there.

Your shadow sometimes calls me
With words that bring me rest
And with its presence lulls me
To a peace that God has blessed.

# SUNLIGHT

The sunlight plays its little game
Dancing on the floor.
It spreads its heat like a clear flame
Upon my waiting door.

It dances with the trees and birds
And shares its energy
With all the creatures on the earth
In a ballet fantasy.

## YOUR RING

Your ring is on my finger
Like a brand upon my heart
And causes you to linger
In my mind while we're apart.

I'll see your soul beside me
In the middle of the night.
Your breath will softly touch me
And set my skin alight.

Memories of our dancing
Through the moments of our life
Or smiling, touching, glancing
When you chose me as your wife.

Someday we'll be pondering
On days that are now gone
And in that minute wandering
In a world beyond this one.

# INFINITY

I saw the moon at midnight shining on the wall.
On my cheek I felt the cooling breath of fall.
I listened for the soft sounds from the waving trees
And the scent of damp ground wafting on the gentle
breeze.

The quiet and the dark brought to me some rest
And I welcomed easy calm as my honored guest
As I stared upon the stars up in the nighttime sky
And looked to them to answer where and what and
why.

Was there a clear solution in my evening view
The final one including this world and me and you?
Or maybe just a clue to the future that will be
When all the world and both of us become infinity?

## MY MATCH

I found my match on this old earth
I walked with him for years
We knew the joy of our son's birth
Shared laughter, love and tears.

He was my help in times of pain.
And sometimes made me cry.
He showed his love for me so plain.
He held my hand and made me sigh.

He showed he had a heart of gold
And made me feel I was his treasure
I thought that we would both grow old
And share this world together.

But now he's gone and I am here
And I miss him every day
And wish that he was oh so near
In each and every way.

## THE ANGEL

I saw the angel sitting in the chair
I smiled at him and asked why he was there.
He looked at me and shrugged his wings
And told the truth about so many things.

He said that when the sky is bright
God is there in the middle of that light
Laughing, singing, having fun
With all his creatures in the sun.

And when there is a velvet dark
God is thinking of the lark
And the song it will sing when it wakes
That song of life and the turns it takes.

Then when there is a pouring rain
God is at your window pane
Tapping, tapping on the glass
Telling you that all things pass.

Then the angel made a move to rise
And looked at me with golden, burning eyes
He said God cares for you in every way
And you should feel his warm love everyday.

When the ground is white with snow
God will always let you know
That spring brings life and love
With amazing blessings from above.

And with that he left me there
With all these thoughts for me to share
When anyone needs to believe
That these are joys they can receive.

# LOVE'S LOSS

My ears were deaf, my eyes were blind.
No one could reach my blacked-out mind.
I was in shock from my love's loss
It was a gulf I could not cross.

I couldn't accept that he was gone
After he left me to travel on
Without his smile to cheer my days
I felt that I was in a haze.

I walked in fog for quite a while
With my heart in a cold exile.
When the warmth returned to me
I felt sheer pain in memory.

But now the ache is dull and deep
And a secret I cannot keep.
It bubbles up without a warning
As searing, loving, screaming mourning.

## I MISS SO MUCH

In his voice I heard his laughter,
In his eyes, a smiling gleam.
We always treasured each moment after
The beginning of our shared dream.

There was a smile, a look, a touch
A way of easy, tender fun.
The teasing I now miss so much
Was like the glowing summer sun.

We took such care of one another
When the world was not so sweet.
Each one would fill the other
To make our world complete.

I miss so much the joking smile
The deep and loving tones
Used in his own free, easy style
That warmed me to my bones.

# SPRING PEACE

Flowers are the heralds of spring
Promising a vivid and scented time
When all the wild birds love to sing
And match the church bells as they chime.

And maybe the sky is heavenly blue
With a sun so bright it makes you blink
And the smell of clover comes to you
As you enjoy a lemony drink.

And time stands still for just the now
So you believe in fantasy
And close your eyes and make a vow
To not forget this ecstasy.

# LIFE'S MAZE

My dog is right here at my feet
And the busy day is winding down.
The routine work is all complete
And I have put on an old nightgown.

I sit here in the evening glow.
And think of simple days gone by,
Of places and people I used to know.
Then there's a deep breath and a sigh.

I see the world so different now
A view from farther down the road.
No need to question where and how
All the speeding now has slowed.

Life is such a strange rat race.
Ever moving as in a maze
Sometimes at such a frantic pace.
But often in a daze.

# PLANNING

Planning for the future
Brings memories of the past
Tomorrow's coming sooner
Nothing seems to last.

Today's a time of chaos
Not knowing what to do
Because my plan was way off
And, of course, included you.

But you are now a memory
A pattern in my brain
A sudden burst of energy
That might bring joy or pain.

## LOVE AND FAMILY

The red rose is the flower of love
With that crimson, velvety look
Brought to life by the sun above
Ending up in a big old book.

But the symbol of family is the tree
It grows for years and spreads wide
With branches growing wild and free
Like relatives on every budding side.

Each rose fades so quickly and it's done
Like July fireworks in the night sky
But the tree lives on in the golden sun
Sturdy and strong and reaching high.

# CHILDHOOD

When I was a child the sky seemed so blue
The grass seemed so cool and green
And in my house I'd wait for you
Watching through the screen.

The sun would shine so hot and bright
And I would suddenly sneeze
Surrounded by that white hot light
And waiting all at ease.

And you would come and play with me.
Then the world would all be right
Because it was my friend and me
Laughing and playing 'til night.

# GAMES

We learn to play games while we're young
And how to try and win.
And the taste of snowflakes on our tongue
As Mom yells "get back in!"

And we run circles round the yard
And play a game of tag.
Then we push and run and try so hard
We dodge and zig and zag.

Then jumping rope on the sidewalk
Until we're out of breath
And then we talk and talk and talk
And talk our moms to death.

# SPARK


Time is all mixed up in my mind:
The future and the past
It's not a thing that's always kind.
We're not meant to last.

Our childhood makes us what we are
And leaves a special mark.
Sometimes a kiss, sometimes a scar,
Our individual spark.

That flicker gives us our own glow
That others recognize.
When I look at you it will show
As a glimmer in your eyes.

# HALF MY HEART

I'm missing half my heart today
As you have gone ahead.
I know you are not far away
But hiding close instead.

Are you in the still air all around?
Or maybe in the bright light?
Are you in that little sound
Or in the dark, dark night?

I feel your spirit close to me
Though I cannot touch your hand.
You're like the breeze I cannot see
As it blows across the sand.

# EACH INSTANT

I fell for his blue eyes.
I fell for his smile.
I should have been wise.
And waited a while.

But the moments were precious
The seconds were gold
They had a real freshness
Not faded and old.

We held on to each instant
We had a good run
It was so important
Our time in the sun.

Don't tell me a secret.
Don't tell me he's gone.
Don't let me regret
All the things left undone.

# TRY AGAIN

Did you love me back then?
Was I special to you?
If you saw me again
What would you do?

Tell me of our love story.
Tell me of the fun days.
Tell me not to worry
About your old and easy ways.

Could we ever try again?
Could it ever work today,
That thing that might have been
Or should I back away?

## FEELING

I close my eyes and see his face
And hear his laugh and tone.
It seems so natural in this place
Where we were often alone.

I feel that simple melting joy
That tender, tingling feeling
I've known since we were girl and boy
And sometimes left me reeling.

My body takes a shuddering gasp.
With that the moment's gone.
My memories torn from my grasp
And I'm left all alone.

# RIDING THE WIND

The lazy heat attacks my senses
I weave and swerve among the flowers
Bordered by the whitewashed fences.
Here I dance and play for hours.

A bird comes toward me from the right
But I move back and to my left
Behind a pole that's painted white
My movements swift, skillful, deft.

My wings are open wide. I'm gliding,
Sailing through the clear, blue sky.
Then dipping, slowing, turning, riding
The wind because I'm a butterfly.

# INNER LIGHT


I sit on the porch in the cool night air
With a warm glow deep inside
And feel a heavy step on the stair.
I watch the door swing wide.

A light flows out past the creaking door
Shining upon my smooth cold skin
Then makes shadows dance all the more
As the door swings closed again

But my flickering inner light still escapes
From my crooked grin in a pattern
Of crazy, wavering, spooky shapes
As I am a Jack-o-lantern .

# KEEP ON

Life can be such a beautiful thing
With your love walking there by your side.
Every day there's a song to sing
And life seems a glorious ride.

But life comes without any guarantee
And will change in the blink of an eye
Then your life will no longer be happily free
And your time will come to cry.

But take a breath and keep on trying
Because you never know your fate
And a day that starts with tears and crying
May end in a perfect state.

# BLINDED

My vision, my touch are muffled now
I move as in a swirling mist
I cannot find my balance now
But stumble, trip and twist.

There was a time when all seemed right.
The path was clear and straight.
A longed for goal appeared in sight
But now it seems too late.

Since I have lost my chosen love
Fog has blinded my eyes.
I look for guidance from above
To make the thick haze rise.

# THE OPPOSITES

The singing and crying, the good and the bad
You feel each one deeper because of the other
Your laughter is louder because you were sad.
Laughter and sadness are sister and brother.

The opposites in life are a pendulum swing
They follow each other like a dog and a cat
Like the words of a lullaby your mother would sing
And an agreement that turns into a spat.

We start out as young and turn into old.
And our minds once so sharp turn dull.
The summertime warmth turns to winter so cold
And whatever goes up must fall.

For usually in dark we find our rest
While in light we run our race.
Hate will ruin our life's quest
But love will give us grace.

# PAST YEARS

The moon is in the sky so bright.
My pillow wet with tears
I cannot find any sleep tonight
I'm wandering through past years.

I see the ones who gave me joy
Walking through my head
My mom, my dad, my pets, my boy
Remembering what was said.

Some are now forever gone
The ones I'll see no more.
And right now I feel all alone
Beyond a long-closed door.

# THE SHELL

I walked along the shore today
Feeling the smooth cool sand.
And watched the palm trees gently sway
While all the world seemed grand.

Looking down I saw a perfect shell
A treasure from the sea.
I picked it up as in a spell
And took it home with me.

Held in my hand my special find
Seemed like it gave me power.
I felt it touch my soul and mind
And turned each minute to an hour.

The shell took me to yesterday,
To old friends that I knew,
To happy days, to fun and play,
And favorite places, too.

And then I woke and looked around.
And all was quiet there
With just a shell upon the ground
As I sat still in my chair.

# BITS OF STAR

Starlight and sunlight are the same thing.
Our stars are suns faraway.
Their light and their heat make the universe sing
As they go through their travels each day.

Reflections of sunlight make planets shine bright
And our moon shine down on me.
Showing me intricate dances of light
And a beautiful night to see.

You and me are made of bits of star
That ended up on earth
And we both traveled very far
Before our earthly birth.

# NIGHT TREES

I listened to the trees tonight whistling in the wind
Nodding and bowing to the stars and clouds
And to a moon whose golden face grinned.

A gentle rain came and rustled softly in the leaves
It fell on down to the thirsty ground
And tap-tapped on the still, solid eaves.

And then there came a silence, a quiet, quiet time
With the tall trees seeming to listen
Until clocks began their morning chime.

# SEASON'S CHEER

A Christmas pine is in the hall.
It's that time of year.
It's standing straight and tall
Full of the season's cheer.

There are glass balls upon the tree
Red and yellow, green and blue
Each one special to me
And a gift from me to you.

Upon the tree the twinkling lights,
A star of sparkling gold,
Reminding all of Christmas sights
Enchanting young and old.

# WINTERTIME

The cold comes in and makes me shiver.
It covers my world with a gray, gray glow.
The winter light sparkles on the river
And a sharp, whipping wind begins to blow.

The time has come for gloves and boots
For scarves and hats and warmer clothes,
Time to listen to the lonely owl's hoots,
And favorite winter songs and shows.

And when the snow brings its wintry bite
And I need furry earmuffs on my head
Maybe I'll hibernate for a night
In a warm and snuggly bed.7

# FAR AND WIDE

I kissed the fabled Blarney Stone
And slept by the Sea of Galilee,
Spent a night on a Russian train
And walked beside the River Dee.
I stood and strolled through ancient Troy.
The Acropolis was a special joy.
I took a Jack the Ripper tour
And in Paris went to Sacre Coeur.

I saw Cappadocia from a balloon
And gazed upon the Mona Lisa.
I took a train from Victoria Station
And saw the Leaning Tower of Pisa.
Stonehenge made me gasp in awe
And I've testified in a court of law.
I've ridden the London Underground
And followed tour guides round and round.

Through it all it's never enough.
There's always something more to see
Swan Lake in St. Petersburg,
Near Jericho there was this tree.
There's Cairo on the river Nile
And tango Buenos Aires style,
San Francisco's Golden Gate,
Bourbon Street, boy that was great!

I have traveled far and wide
And done so many things.
I've visited museums, glaciers
And homes of ancient kings.
I've walked across the dark, dark moors,
Caught fish with Grandpa's fishing lures.
I've seen things I never thought I'd see
In places I never thought to be.

# MISSING YOU

Cotton candy clouds are floating across the sky.
The trees are whispering softly why, why, why.
Their background is such a perfect lightened
turquoise blue.
And here I sit with aching thoughts missing talks
with you.

Bo, our dog, you left with me is full of faithful love.
I wonder if you see us from somewhere up above
He looks at me with trusting, begging big brown
eyes.
And do you laugh with joy when it's your place
where Bo lies.

I face the future now you see in our once shared
home.
Your belongings catch and hold my eyes in their
hungry roam.
There is a lost and lonely feel in moving on these
days.
And I arise and sadly touch your things that hold my
gaze.

# A PART OF ME

Sometimes when I wake my very soul is grey
And you're not with me there to brighten up my day.
I look around me in a fog...a sad and lonely haze.
I need a spark, a light, a glowing fire to wake me from my
daze.

And then there comes a memory.  One moment that we
shared.
And suddenly it lifts me up to remember how you cared.
Then I can feel a shot pulsing through my veins
Flowing, pouring, rushing, like the springtime rains.

You are still a part of me.  A mainstay of my being.
Everyday I feel you there affecting what I'm seeing.
What we had will always be in my life and heart
And you and I will ever be a whole to never part.

# HEALED


The night was just so freezing cold.
The wind was sharp and shrill and bold.
I snuggled in my furry hood
And shook for moments where I stood.

That night I felt that evening chill
Like snow upon my windowsill.
I hugged my warm, warm coat to me
And thought of a warming cup of tea.

But I needed the winter to bring me to life
To cut through my misery like a knife.
So I walked through the brown and frosty field
And asked God that my aching heart be healed.

## THANKSGIVING

We sit around a table and fold our hands in prayer.
We say a grateful thanks for friends and family there.
The feast today is special.  All our favorite things.
Prepared in just the perfect way. A spread that's fit
for kings.

Right now that doesn't matter.  There's no need to
impress.
We just share these simple moments that bring us
happiness.
There's potatoes, gravy, turkey, stuffing, pumpkin
pie.
When all of us have eaten, all we can do is sigh.

Then sounds and smells around us bring back
yesteryear
And our hearts fill up with memories.  In every eye a
tear.
We miss those voices from the past that are not here
today.
The people that we love so much that have now gone
away.

# TOGETHER, TOO

I saw the clothes I wore that day.
They're in a closet - put away.
They brought all the memories back
In a raging, roaring blitz attack.

I felt his touch upon my arm.
A flow of feeling sweet and warm
Running, singing through my veins
 Like swiftly moving summer rains.

I could not think, could only feel.
As we moved close, my life so real.
That was the start of what I knew
Would be our life together, too.

# MY OASIS

I gaze at the fire in front of me blazing oh so bright.
It gives off an ever-welcoming heat that warms me through
the night.
The flickering flames lick at their fuel like a thirsting dog.
And outside it's so cold and damp with a rising fog.

Part of this room is real, of course, and part is just a mirage.
A space that's partly in this world and partly a movie
montage.
The fireplace isn't there, you see, just sometimes on a screen.
But in my mind it's just as true as anyplace you have seen.

Yet in this room is my oasis of safety and warmth and calm.
Here I may read a favorite book or maybe an enriching psalm.
This place has become a den of sweet and loving joy-
An enchanted spot where I can be with the things that I enjoy.

# MISS YOU, MY DEAR

Where are you, my darling?
Where are you, my love?
I looked for you all over.
You're all I can think of.

I feel your sweet spirit.
I know you are here.
When you are not with me
I miss you, my dear.

The angels are lucky,
Entertained by your smile.
I wish I could see it
If just for a while.

# RESOLUTIONS

I walked into Bethlehem through the border wall
Though the shock of its existence is something I
recall.
We think of love and star and of a virgin birth
But where and when and how will there be peace on
Earth?

The sacred place did fill me with hope and peace and
awe
But even that did not make up for some things that I
saw.
The little town had tension that one does not expect.
Why can't people treat each other with sincere
respect?

And so today I plead with you, all my friends who
read this
Stand tall in love and unity because we really need
this.
So, please remember sharing can bring both parties
cheer.
The world can be a lonely place when caring is not
here.

These are just my thoughts, a poem of my prayers.
But I ask for your support anyone who dares
To try to make a better world, free of hate and fear
And make these resolutions to start the brand new year.

## CONNECTED

When we met, we were both searching and raw.
Far from complete.  Not recognizing what we saw
In front of us - in one another that was familiar.
But each one was reaching. The quest similar.

We measured each other with talk and smile
Looking for connection all the while.
And suddenly recognition was there
That we two could find many things to share.

Each moved forward with give and take.
Honing ourselves for our futures sake.
Until we found the secret key
That connected and locked you and me.

# RELATIVE TO NOW

The sun has hidden behind a cloud.
The day has lost its laughter.
I say a favorite prayer aloud.
What can life be like after?

Time is a thought undefined.
When I try my future to see
Relative to now is all I find.
I am not the same me as I will be.

And when I look at my own past.
I became such a different me,
I find that that I did not last.
Is that really a me I see?

CARING


I heard the bells ring pure and sweet
From the belfry of the church at the end of the
street.
The air was crisp and clear and cold
The music, the melodies from days of old.

It brought a beauty back to me
Of the days when a small town seemed like family,
Together in help and peace and love
Looking for guidance from a power above.

Today that peace seems far away,
Lost in the negatives that have all in sway.
Do not choose to follow this crowd.
Speak the truth and say it aloud.

We need caring sister and brother,
Always love for our mother, always love for each
other.
And when we keep this goal in mind.
Always love for all mankind.

# TO SARAH AND CLIFF ON HER BIRTHDAY


Sarah and Cliff have been through times so tough
But together have made it through the rough
Of the beautiful and tender life they share
With such hard work and gentle care.

And in their eyes and smiles I've seen
How close and happy they have been.
Each a support to the other one.
Every day better than the day that's gone.

So now with Christmas coming soon,
They can sit under the silver moon
To dream fine dreams of their coming days
And know that their love can last always.

# CHRISTMAS ANGEL

A Christmas angel watches me
High above my Christmas tree.
He gives me wishes, hope and cheer
And helps me make it through the year.

He has a sweet and lovely smile
In a fine cherubic style.
And there's that dimple in his cheek
Right before he starts to speak.

In his eye there is that twinkle.
His nose has just that little crinkle.
I know he's special.  It's so true!
He's known as Santa Claus to you.

# REJOICE

I close my eyes and I am free
Of all that has been worrying me.
In my mind I hear a voice.
A soothing whisper says "Rejoice".

"If you will let me in this night,
I will bring you my special light
That will free you of doubt and tears
Bringing peace and calming fears."

"Rejoice, I am the spirit in you
Leading the way to all that's true.
Taking away the pain you are feeling.
Leading you to a sacred healing."

# BLIZZARD

I see a snowflake drifting by.
One single snowflake in the sky.
And then a trillion snowflakes follow
Drifting in that little hollow.

It is a miracle of white,
A special glowing silver sight.
A drop of water once so clear
Changed to lace by the atmosphere.

Then there comes a muffling blizzard
As if led by a master wizard
Performing a pure and blinding christening
Leaving the forest cold and glistening.

# THIS SUMMER FLOWER

A stem and leaf come from a seed
Breaking through the soil and freed
From its sleep and onto earth.
What a miracle of birth!

All life is like this summer flower
Blooming, changing by the hour.
Struggling, striving to attain
Steady growth from sun and rain.

Its time is short but brings us joy
Often a gift to a girl from her boy.
A sweet memento of their love
And of the future that's dreamt of.

## ALL MEANT TO BE

Tell me the stories.  Tell me the rhymes.
Give me a gift of your remembered times.
All of those days that meant so much to you.
A picture of history that you know to be true.

Mother and father to daughter and son
Share with and tell them how all things were
done.
It's good to remember and build on the past
And have known traditions as few things do last.

But as we move forward take into account
That the paths that we choose, the stairs that we
mount,
Must make us all equal and better and free
Because that is the way we were all meant to be.

# MY CUP OF TEA


Tea the oriental drink.
Makes me feel quite in the pink.
It's a sip from heaven's feast.
A taste of nectar at the least.

The delicate, blooming hints teas bring
To taste buds is a magic thing.
It can help your senses savor
Your life and give it special flavor.

Tonight I shall have my cup of tea
And dream of things as they could be.
A world with all its infinite views
And finally just the way I choose.

# I WILL FIGHT

Life is not always a pretty thing.
We cannot know what it will bring.
When we have lost, as we often lose,
Our next step is for us to choose.

Will we give up or will we fight?
Will we seek to do what's right?
I can't know what you will choose
But I will fight and take a bruise.

I will dig and make my stand
And claw for right with my bare hand.
And when the struggle is over and done
I truly hope that we've all won.

# YOU ARE MY TOWER OF STRENGTH

When will my pride go away?
When will the time come to say
All of those things that are good
Without a thought of whether I should?

It's hard to give away power
Even though you are my tower
Of strength when I need it so much
From your heart and your gentle sweet touch.

But now that I've left my first youth
I know it's now time for this truth.
You have always helped me succeed
By supporting me with faith, word and deed.

## THESE POEMS

These poems knock upon my head
And pull me out of my lazy bed
Begging for my full attention
With words with just the right intention.

Sometimes they come from deep inside
And sometimes they're from far and wide.
But always they require my thought
So just the right images are caught.

They make me see a special world
Where this and that are totally swirled
Together in a spinning vision
Described in such complete precision.

# FAST AND EVER FURIOUSER

I view the world as ever curiouser
With this and that being strange.
It moves so fast and ever furiouser
From change to change to change.

I cannot find a comfortable place
To rest and get my breath each day
But am always in the crazy chase
Hoping to find a calmer way.

If my mind could have some peaceful moments
After passing through a secret door,
I'd arrive at a place of healing silence
And a joy that means much more.

# MY VALENTINE

You were mine, my Valentine.
Wrapping me with joy and love.
All your smiles were just a sign
Like the purist pearl white dove.

There was sometimes worry
And painful moments shared.
The times that I was sorry,
But still you knew I cared.

Today the past is present
Within my beating heart.
A moment sweet and silent
Remembering our start.

## DROWNING IN SWEET PAIN

I sit here in the silence
Drowning in sweet pain.
Drinking in the cool scents
Of a morning rain.

Today is just beginning.
Yesterday is gone.
Tomorrow I may be winning
When I look out on the dawn.

But now is where I start
To move from and build upon
So I must find the heart
To step forward and go on.

# ENCOURAGED

Trying hard is harder trying
Just right now I feel like crying
I started today with so much hope
But now I'm fighting an internal "nope".

But I look up and see a light
And am encouraged by the sight.
Why would I sit here and sigh?
Yes, I can mount another try.

I who've had so many wins
See no reason I can't win again.
Just like before, there's no guarantee.
But, watch out world you can't stop me!

# THAT CHILD

Life is a fabric woven with dreams
And starlight and rainbows and glowing
moonbeams.
That is the way I saw the world then
When I was a young child of maybe just ten.

As I grew older and faced more of life
And saw in the world all the meanness and strife,
It seemed my existence lost some of its beauty.
I found in it much more of hard work or duty.

But that child is not gone.  She peeks out at times.
And skips through the world and whistles and
rhymes.
She sings in the shower and when she is driving.
And all of those times she seems to be thriving.

# POT OF SHIMMERING GOLD

A handsome man in green was there standing on the hill.
He looked at me and tipped his hat saying "Come, my
name is Will.
I will help you with your wishes and make your dreams
come true.
If you will dance a jig with me right in the morning dew."

Just then from far away I heard a magic melody
That seemed to move me in a dance with not a thought
from me.
And there we were the two of us swaying as a pair
An intricate, exciting dance that we performed right there.

The wind whipped up and suddenly the trees were
dancing, too.
The moment seemed enchanted, full of something new.
Everything looked bigger or were we getting small?
It seemed that we were suddenly hardly there at all.

And as we faded into the misty morning haze
I looked around and saw things in a foggy daze.
Other dancing couples were swirling all around
What seemed to be a glowing entrance in the dewy ground.

At that opening stood a pot of shimmering gold,
Glimmering, shining, beckoning, a legend bright and bold.
And then I danced right past it thinking that beyond it was
my dream.
But of course the shiny things in life aren't always what
they seem.

## DEEP DOWN INSIDE

The song in my heart is silent today.
The sky seems cloudy and gray.
My senses have numbed, overloaded
As the pain of emotion exploded.

Deep down inside me I'm lost
Now life has exacted its cost
For the deep love and joy that I've known
And the happiness that I've been shown.

But knowledge comes from those times of my past
That showed my possibilities are vast.
The times I was all alone
Then discovered a strength all my own.

## PRAYER FOR PEACE

God, please hold me in your hand.
Help me heal and walk and stand.
When I feel the task's too long,
Let me know that I am strong.

God, please hold me close at night.
Lead me toward the morning light.
Tend me through my midnight tears
Often caused by lonely fears.

God, please whisper to my heart
And tell me how to be a part
Of the changes we all must make
To help bring peace in your **name's** sake.

# A POEM PERCOLATING


There's a poem percolating searching for a rhyme.
Word after word popping just in time.
Creating such an intricate, special, singing verse
Sometimes for praise, sometimes for joy, sometimes as a curse.

Poetry should always be a way that we all can share
Special thoughts and feelings showing how we care.
You and I are different, but in so many ways the same.
Words can come out right when it is not just a game.

If you like their words and they can make you feel
Something that is new, something that may heal.
Then is it possible that we can meet right here
In poetry with words of hope and let go of our fear?

# WRONG OR RIGHT

We talk of how we see the world..
Of what is wrong or right.
But isn't it how the world sees us
That worries us at night?

Many people know what's right
And speak of it to friends.
But when it comes to standing firm
Their friends is where it ends.

Sometimes it takes such courage
To stand for what you believe
Rather than take a chance on the
Disapproval you might receive.

# SOMETHING FROM A DREAM

In a quiet oak forest
There flowed a gentle stream
Right into a small blue lake
Like something from a dream.

By the lake lived a young lass
Full of hopes and fears
She lived a life like most girls
Full of laughter and tears.

Then one day she met a lad
Who made her heart beat fast
Bringing love into her world
As if a spell was cast.

Together the lad and lass
Chose each other to wed.
So there beside the rippling lake
A lovely life they led.

# MEMORY OF A TREAT

Today my mind was wondering
Through moments tender and sweet.
I was searching for a special time -
A memory of a treat.

And suddenly there it was
In my minds eye
That special day, that special minute
When I could only sigh.

The beauty of it all!
How much we felt and cared!
I hope you understand
But the rest just can't be shared.

## TO PAULA

For me, Paula, you hold such a special place.
Thank you for your smiling face!
I won't forget your loving care
And how for me you're always there.

I look back at all the things we've done.
So many times of joy and fun.
But there's been times of sadness, too.
When you have let me lean on you.

We have a unique sister bond.
I'm in your corner beyond beyond.
When you need help or love or cheer
I hope you know that I am here.

## CHOICES

Life is full of many choices
Argued by conflicting voices.
You may say this is right.
That it's as clear as day and night.

But I can see the other side
What another's point of view might hide.
Or maybe something that's hard to see
Because you think it just can't be.

So when I think I know what's true
I have to choose what's best to do.
And once I've chosen how I'll live,
If you can't agree, please forgive.

WHEN YOU LOOK BACK


Forgive yourself for what is past.
It's over now.  The die is cast.
If you have done the best you knew,
There may be nothing you can do.

When you look back remember, too,
You have a new and different view.
Be gentle with yourself today
As you learn and grow from day to day.

But looking back should give you a chance
To see your choices and enhance
The way you make any new decision
By using a wiser, tempered vision.

# DIFFERENT VIEWS

Forgiving others who care for you
May not be so hard to do.
Then there's those you've found uncaring
Not a relationship worth repairing.

Me? If I can step into their shoes,
Maybe see from different views
What caused the hurt and pain I feel
I can choose to let it heal.

Might we both have been unfair
When we didn't see both sides in the glare
Of the tears from the hurt we were feeling.
Now can we forgive as part of healing?

# FAITH AND WILL


Faith is that voice inside me that I cannot shake.
Sensation speaking within me bringing me awake
Singing through my veins in an eternal recognition
Of the moments giving me a full, clear, inner vision.

I believe that sometimes what will be will be.
But that sometimes success is solely up to me.
And in some old tomes from creaky dusty shelves
I have read that God helps those who help
themselves.

So much of life is dictated by our faith and will.
Without competing motives our lives might just
stand still.
But when we mix with others and stir with nature,
too
Life becomes a work of art starring me and you.

# THE GARDEN OF GETHSEMANE

In the garden of Gethsemane
By an old, old olive tree.
I felt emotion in the air
Of all those things that happened there.

Fear, betrayal, acceptance, too,
Since Christ knew then what he must do
To bring the ultimate fulfillment of
His healing mission of pure, sweet love.

So for all the souls that he could save
He took his steps knowing he gave
More to them than they could know.
The eternal treasure only he could bestow.

# GOD WEPT

God wept today in mighty tears
That fell from out of the skies.
Maybe He felt the pain that sears
When a loved one dies.

Might He have been feeling the agony
That all of us have known
When He knew that no action He
Could take would erase a single groan?

While I could not see His face,
His mood was somber and gray
As if from a far distant place
He held himself at bay.

It seemed the turmoil raged in Him
That He had set this way
For man to be brought to Him
And saved on judgement day.

## WORDS TO HEAL

Rising at the break of dawn.
Walking in the morning dew.
All my painful doubt is gone
With the early breeze that blew.

I can feel the sun upon me.
I can smell the sweet spring air.
The world right now is not as lonely
Knowing we have love we share.

You have taken our hands to hold.
You have spoken words to heal.
And now our world is not so cold.
You have brought a warmth we feel.

## MEMENTOS AND MEMORIES

Mementos and memories,
Pictures on the wall.
Bring back special stories!
Oh, yes! I recall!

Things we did together
When we were much younger.
Playing all our games
With a youthful hunger.

Fueled by just a glance
A visit to the past.
The cheapest form of travel
And it can be a blast!

## SACRED WOOD

I walked into the sacred wood to free my mind
from pain.
The day had been a hard one and I was very
stressed.
I hoped the natural beauty would make me feel
more sane
And help relieve the tightening, the ache within
my breast.

The moon was like a searchlight glowing in the sky
Making velvet shadows of soaring bats and birds.
The magic of the fireflies flit, flit, flitting by
Added to an atmosphere I can't describe in words.

The wind blew through the trees causing them to
dance.
With waving leaves and bowing limbs moving
with such grace
As if they heard a special tune that put them in a
trance.
What a night!  What a spell in that enchanted
place!

# THE COOLING SOLACE

I heard a voice calling to me
Upon a flowery hill.
Nature making a gentle plea
While all seemed suddenly still.

The words were soft and tender,
A salve to ease my pain.
A gift God chose to render
With a soft and healing rain.

I felt the cooling solace
And heard the words of light
Awakening colors to fullness
To unveil a vibrant sight.

A world that an ache had hidden
From eyes that could not see
Became a beautiful garden
Where I was suddenly free.

# MY MOM

When I see a flitting butterfly,
I see my mom in my mind's eye.
Mom loved those and peacocks, too
And most of the animals in the zoo.

She loved old movie films and stars.
And all those old fantastic cars.
She loved relatives I'd rarely seen
And being treated like a queen.

She loved her pets, dog or cat,
A good old long, long cozy chat,
With a cup of steaming tea
While sitting with friends and family.

## SOMEONE UNIQUE


Moment to moment I dance with my past
Remembering a beauty I hoped was to last.
Minute to minute I search for the words
To describe every picture my memory hoards.

Hour to hour I smile at the thought
That my tongue might describe a vision I caught.
Day to day habits repeating in time
Like the sound of a clock's familiar old chime.

Year after year seeing patterns repeat
Like pole after pole of lights on a street.
Second to second a surprise in my view
Someone unique.  Someone like you!

## HONORED HEROES


Ghosts of our honored heroes
Stand tall within our hearts
As in each eye a tear grows
And within a deep pain starts.

These men were lost to loved ones,
Fighting for our beloved country.
Forever lost to future dawns
Beyond some dark and foreign sea.

Placing medals on each hero's chest
Like shining stars on a dark night sky.
We lay these patriots to eternal rest
Thanking the moral code they lived by.

# VICTORIOUS

Pain and suffering are never easy.
Waking to a new day weak and queasy.
Reaching out for any hope.
Searching, praying you can cope.

Feeling days march slowly, achingly by
Knowing each move could make you cry.
Or maybe relief will come tonight
And a promised cure will make you right.

Whether an illness of body or soul
It all can take such a terrible toll.
And it might take all you have in you
To be victorious and start anew.

## OUR FIGHT

I took a breath and looked around.
The world it hardly made a sound
As I chose the path that I would take,
Would I shatter? Would I break?

Fighting for each and every win
My chances just so very thin.
He took my hand and held it tight
Helping me to win our fight.

I now go forward on my own.
Still on my path but now alone.
For both of us I take a stance
For both of us I will advance.

## PROLOGUE TO CAMPING DAY

My friend Paula and I and some other friends went
camping over a weekend.  As a note Bo is my lovely,
sweet, calm Bluetick Coonhound, an absolute
sweetheart and connoisseur.


## CAMPING DAY

The sunlight chased us round the camp
Like fireflies waking in the evening light
It chased away the cold and damp
Making the day seem just about right.

Every meal was a celebratory feast
With smoke-flavored foods on every dish.
Added to that there was Bo the beast
Looking for treats to fulfill his wish.

At times we sat near the fire and chatted
About times gone by and people we'd known
Or played card games and laughed and spatted.
Then came the dusk and the starlight shone.

# WITH THANKS

Listen close and hear the day,
All the things that come your way...
Traffic, children, planes and birds,
Dogs and cats and loving words.

Can you smell life in the air,
Cotton candy at a fair
Rain and dew and new mown grass,
Sweet perfume on a pretty lass?

Look and see the sky above,
The picture of someone you love,
A flower reaching toward the sun,
Beloved children having fun.

You are blessed to have these things,
To savor these gifts that this day brings.
So smile with thanks as you read my verse
And enjoy the abundance of the universe.

# FEELING COLORS

What do colors mean to you?
Do you choose purple or maybe true blue?
Do you long for a brilliant red?
Or maybe crimson stops you dead?

When the sky is grey and very dreary
Do you feel like you are just so weary?
But with a turquoise hue above
Do your thoughts turn to things you love?

Does lemon yellow wake  your senses?
Does the world look better through rose-colored
lenses?
Does a green, green lawn make you feel alive
And ready to go and win and thrive?

Black and white are stark and true
Like plain speaking between me and you.
But your daily life would lose such texture
Without each moment's color mixture.

## THE SUN BEAMS


I look at the sky. It looks like fall.
But the calendar shows it's not at all.
Summer should be here, you see.
Only it seems cool and wet to me.

Water's standing all around.
Muddy puddles and rain abound.
Everything has a muted hue.
The dullness dims my spirits, too.

Another moment the sun beams out.
The grass is the green I dream about,
The sky a blue, majestic sight.
A world changed by that radiant light.

# IN MY MIND

As memories and tears arise
I take a breath and close my eyes.
I hope to find a place of peace
So the pain within my heart will cease.

Days with him are close to me.
The things we shared are what I see...
Our home, our pets, our laughter, too,
And how our life together grew.

He is still here in my mind.
Filling thoughts of every kind.
And while he's there I feel his love
Coming to me from up above.

# CELEBRATE OUR FREEDOMS

We celebrate our freedoms
From emperors and kingdoms,
From those who would oppress us,
And find ways to suppress us.

Those who trade in peddling lies
And spread their hate by slanted cries
That undermine our unity
Are seeking to destroy our community.

I offer this warning thought
A story told by a liar oft-caught
Must be accompanied by proof
Not just much-repeated spoof.

We say truth sets us free.
And I am sure we all agree
That lies destroy our pacts.
That we must demand the facts.

## INDEPENDENCE DAY

Celebrate independence, now!
Crowds, parades and fireworks! Wow!
Flags are flying all around!
What a feast of sight and sound!

Picnic tables loaded, lots of food.
People in a patriotic mood.
Children playing in the park
Waiting for the show at dark.

Then comes the glowing rockets' glare
Leaving smoke snakes in the air.
And lighting all the land with flashes
Followed by frightful booms and crashes.

## NOT IN OUR CONTROL


You may try all that you can
To follow just your perfect plan.
And you may think that's very wise,
But life may take you by surprise.

Life is full of this and that -
First a dog and then a cat.
You may choose a lonely way.
Then find that love is here to stay.

But life is not in our control.
Do you really want that goal?
On the way what will you lose?
You won't know 'til after you choose.

# PRAY THIS DAY

What kind of future will there be?
By that time will we all be free?
Or will some be dealing with some terror
Surviving day to day with prayer?

All of us should pray this day
Asking for a better way,
A future that is free from fears,
A future  without so many tears.

But we all know this will take work.
That's not a thing that we can shirk.
But, if we move toward these goals,
We may then have saved a million souls.

# WORDS COME TUMBLING

Sometimes words come tumbling
Like a thunderstorm that's rumbling.
They hit the air as if they're springing
As an old song that needs singing.

Have you ever had a rising feeling
That special thoughts from you are spilling?
Rippling, raging like a river
And deep within you quiver.

And once the words have leapt into the air,
You're suddenly without a care.
Because the thoughts were a growing seed
And now are grown and have been freed.

# THE BEAUTY OF LIFE

Looking at the starry night sky
I can imagine lives gone by.
I know when I look at all the stars
I'm looking past loves and lives and wars.

There have been so many stories
Of people doomed by despots and worries
Who struggled and saved the beauty of life
And found their place, free of strife.

I can see that all things pass
And take a moment to lift a glass
To all the ones who've gone before
From hopeless lives to a distant shore.

# METAMORPHOSIS

I watched the magic firebird rising from the ashes.
Thunder boomed and lightning came in split-second
flashes.
Strange, the end of the beginning is the beginning yet
again
A cycle of life many wish they could attain.

Then I wake from my dream and look for its truth.
And find it in life's  many twists and turns up
through my youth
Until the point I'm at right now and on beyond
through ages.
I will change and learn and grow and start many
brand new pages.

I am lucky I can adapt to the many changes time can
bring.
I can hope and try and learn to not only live, but sing.
And with that metamorphosis comes a gentle calm
Knowing that I again can be in comfort...safe and
warm.

# EVERY NEW CONNECTION

In every breath you take you take in part of our
world
And in your lungs and blood the components all are
swirled.
In every look around, your eyes take a surrounding
sampling
Of all the sights nearby, whether standing still or
rambling.

Every time you touch the things within your reach
You learn so many things that only touch can teach.
Have you forgot that feeling when things to you are
new,
And each and every new connection helps you know
what's true?

Opening my senses to all that is always changing
And thereby taking new stock will require major
rearranging
Of all my wishes, thoughts, beliefs and feelings, too
And then I won't be always stuck with a stagnant,
dated view.

## NEED IN SOMEONE'S EYES


Time moves round and round me
Changing all the views I see.
Like a movie on a screen
Moving on from scene to scene.

Sometimes I'm the outsider,
Just a carousel rider.
Looking but not living.
Taking but not giving.

Then life plays it's greatest trick.
I'm drawn right in..oh, so quick.
I can't be cold.  I can't be wise
When I see need in someone's eyes

# GIVE BACK

Yesterday has come and gone.
What have we lost and what have we won?
Will tomorrow be a better day
For you and I?  Who can say?

But we can do the best we can
To be of help to our fellow man.
And give a thought for every minute
With sharing, joy and love in it.

How little it costs to offer a smile
Or give a friend that extra mile.
We should give back to those who give
As a natural part of the way we live.

# Working Hard

Working hard to make a life,
To be the best husband or best wife.
Laboring and trying hard to be
All you can and still be free.

To make your family's life successful
You lose sleep and it's so stressful.
And inside you want your own time,
To not be ruled by a clock alarm chime.

And in the end you wonder if all you do
Is worth the time and effort, too.
But then that feeling of warmth and care
Comes to you and yours when you all share.

# OUT OF THE CAVES

Man and woman from the start of time
Out of the caves was quite a climb!
Wind and rain, fire and flame
Part of the world from which we came.

We are all connected here.
All a part of a small blue sphere.
Travelling around a glowing star
Have we come so very far?

What can we be?  What have we been?
Full of purity!  Full of sin!
On a trek to what we will be
In that future that none can see.

# A WAY TO EXPRESS

The pitter patter of a special beat
Heart and music in rhythm meet.
The dance moves on from note to note
A unique performance of what one wrote.

A high note here.  A low note there.
Instruments joined in a tune they share.
Lovely stanzas creating a whole
Designed to touch your very soul.

Maybe a drum,  maybe a voice
Joined perhaps as a way to rejoice
Or a way to express each inner feeling
And help us on a path of healing.

# BLESSINGS FROM ABOVE

The things in life we love
Are blessings from above.
Our children give life a glow
As we watch them change and grow.

Some are neighbors and friends
And all those fun old trends.
Remember all the songs of old
The stories that your grandpa told.

And when I think of all things past
It seems that life has gone by so fast.
And left with me some lovely visions
Through its many, many varied seasons.

## SOUL LOOKS INTO SOUL

When eyes meet eyes
In that a magic lies.
Soul looks into soul
And both may see the whole.

When connection's so direct
All our feelings reflect
The need within us all
To remove life's divisive wall.

And hope that we can share
In a way that shows we care
The deep, deep things we feel
When life is so, so real.

# GOD'S PLAN

God talked to Moses from a burning bush.
My friend fell and was saved by a turning bush
She said that when that plant broke her fall,
It  turned her so she wasn't hurt at all.

She was kind of trapped this is true,
But able to make a call for help, too.
If it all hadn't happened this way
There might have been injury.  Who can say?

Nature can be so tricky to man
Maybe both good and bad are God's plan.
And He continues to help you and me
Using his creations with ingenuity.

# SUMMER HAS TURNED

The wind blows through the dark, dark night.
The dancing of clouds blocks the fall moonlight.
There's a crunch of leaves beneath my feet.
The scent of a bonfire makes the spell complete.

Summer has turned to a chilly fall.
In the air there's a great owl's call,
Always a spooky, eerie sign.
A shiver runs right down my spine

When I reach the door and open it wide,
I quickly take a step inside
Craving the warmth that greets me there
And the lights and my comfy, cozy chair.

# SEEK THE TRUTH

Emotion is a human cloud
Creating things we say aloud
Things that are not always true
Steeping to a stronger brew.

Clear that mist from your own mind.
Look for the facts that you can find.
With truth and logic clear your vision
So that your beliefs are based in reason.

With yourself and others be fair.
Seek the truth because you care.
Honesty and truth, you see,
Clear the air and set us free.

# WHAT PEOPLE SAY

People may swear and yell at you
And call you names that are not true.
They may make a point of lurking
Or try to needle you by smirking.

Choose not to care what people say
To solely tear your confidence away
And make you doubt and bully you.
Have the strength to know what's true.

And unless you choose to give them power
You're the one who'll win the hour.
And when you do retain control
You will be one...undivided and whole.

## WHAT MIGHT BE TRUE


Life moves so fast in these modern days.
Technology serves us in many ways.
You can watch your life upon a screen
A high depth original changing scene.

Cameras here and cameras there.
Seeing everything!  When and where...
And if you assume that you know all,
That very assumption becomes a wall.

A blocking of what might be true
Could stop you from a complete clear view.
To make good decisions for your future acts
Be sure to question and consider all the facts.

# DO YOUR DAY'S BEST

Look for facts in all before you.
Use care to say what you know is true.
Even if you're ill and so, so weary
Do your best to say things clearly.

The air is full of gossip and hum.
There may be chatter..chum to chum.
If mumbled whispers should feed your fear,
Best to make your thoughts pure and clear.

Your best may waver when you tire
And may not be at the level you desire.
But if you question and consider what's true
And do your day's best, it's all you can do.

# FOR US AN EARTHLY TREASURE

We are the things we believe in so many ways.
These beliefs were built in us over many, many days.
From our time of birth we learned from all around
us,
With every breath and contact and all that did
surround us.

But we can question now all that filled our early
thoughts
In those first few years as pure and hungry tots.
And, if it is not good for us, we may make the choice
To replace those words and habits with a loving
voice.

We may remove the fears that have taken from us
pleasure.
This could give us joy and love ....for us an earthly
treasure,
A light that we can share in joy with all those that we
touch
And in every way that matters improve our world so
much.

# HALLOWEEN

The witching power of charming spell
Comes from the tone of a magic bell.
It rings sweet and pure on Halloween
Releasing powers, some unseen.

The day brings us near those of our past
Full of memories we wish to last,
Thoughts of the spirits of days gone by
Shared with a tear, a laugh and a sigh.

The night brings masks and treats and tricks,
Costumes and makeup, wigs and broomsticks,
But the next day's dawn will dispell these visions
Leaving but a day full of daily decisions.

## DAY OF THE DEAD


All prepare for the Day of the Dead.
Build your altars to invite those passed
To offer favorite things, drinks and bread,
And for the young souls, toys amassed.

Visit the graves of the loved ones, too.
Celebrate those you lost and love
Remembering them in all you do,
And saying a prayer to powers above.

Give tribute to their unique worth
And help those who feel adrift.
Celebrate with joy their lives on earth
And their every good act and gift.

# WE LIVE IN HOPE

Every day we live in hope
Of this beautiful world's revival.
With bravery and strength we cope
And work toward its survival.

We fight for our loved ones,
Make their safety our duty.
We look forward to new dawns.
And thrill at life's beauty.

Awaken us to all that's needed.
Make our best the goal.
We will know when we've succeeded.
We will feel it in each soul.

## HANDS AND MINDS


I am not just what you see.
There is a world inside of me.
Where it is at times so lonely
And may be true for my eyes only.

With another I can share
Making me much more aware.
As we talk and think and feel
Other things become more real.

Thus many worlds touch each other
And people bond one with another.
Hands and minds can join this way
Bringing to all a better day.

www.ingramcontent.com/pod-product-compliance
Lightning Source LLC
Chambersburg PA
CBHW021408150726
47989CB00005B/2452